What people are saying

"Parenting is hard," I say to myself all the time. When I find myself struggling with parenthood, I am thankful I have Christie's book. I'm not the perfect parent, and this book reminds me that it's okay. It's through God's grace that I gain wisdom on how to handle tough situations. Christie outright said it in her book: "I can only try my best every day—that's all God requires of me." Praise God for this truth!

—Rebecca Coutu
Entrepreneur
friend, and mother of two sons

This incredible book is a mirror to the soul of every mother, father, and human who has ever questioned if God could see them through. It will make you shed a tear, laugh out loud, and shout, "That's me, too!" all at the same time, through Christie's honest and heartwarming stories. The Voice of God is audible, even in the smallest details of every day—a theme Christie so accurately portrays. It will encourage you to believe that even the mundane tasks of life are incredibly significant in the journey to discovering God's heart for you.

—Bernadene Bagalay
Worship Leader
friend, and mother of two young sons

Christie writes this book with all of the rawness and authenticity with which she lives her life. This book is a *must read* for every mother who has questioned her sanity in the midst of child-rearing! Even more so, this book is a must read for every mother who has questioned her faith along the journey, as well. Spoiler alert: Christie is not the perfect mother. Shocker, I know! However, she doesn't strive to be a perfect mother; she strives to be a faithful and obedient child of God. She lives every day in communion with the Holy Spirit, letting Him guide her through the chaos of family life.

This book is not just a template, but a courage booster for how each of us can do that in the unique way that God has called us to in our individual lives. Christie has a way of seeing through impossible situations with eyes of faith that cut through the clutter, even when that clutter includes crayons and crumbs!

—Jessica Sampson
Teacher of the Prophetic
friend, and mother of one daughter

As a new mother, I can relate to the life-changing experience of a tiny human! Christie and her book have reminded me that we can only do our best to keep our family in order, and the rest is in God's hands! Her perseverance of creating a life that works for her and her family had encouraged me to build on my relationship with the Lord, so I, too, can be my best self. I have yet to grow stronger in my walk of faith, and I am truly blessed to have Christie uplift and teach me, as well as others through the multiple places God has guided her to.

—Catherine Amoyo
Entrepreneur
sister-in-law, friend,
and mother of one young boy

Christie Amoyo's book, *Crayons, Crumbs, and Christian Growth,* is a must read for all people of all spiritual levels, as she explores the juggling of life from diapers to daily devotions. You will learn many positive ways to keep your life in balance while gaining from the author's firsthand experiences; this book is a great read for mothers and people just trying to cope with all of life's demands and begin to dream for their own lives once again.

—Carla De Roy-Busby
Founder, The Beauty Box by Sheriff
friend, and mother of four daughters

Crayons, Crumbs, and CHRISTIAN GROWTH

Encouragement
for the Highs and
Lows of Parenthood

Crayons, Crumbs, and CHRISTIAN GROWTH

Christie Amoyo

CRAYONS, CRUMBS, AND CHRISTIAN GROWTH

Printed in Canada

ISBN: 978-1-4866-1714-2

Word Alive Press
119 De Baets Street, Winnipeg, MB R2J 3R9
www.wordalivepress.ca

Cataloguing in Publication may be obtained through Library and Archives Canada

Dedication

I want to dedicate this book to my mother. Not only was she my best friend growing up, but she is also a friend to my children. She has been there beside me throughout all these adventures, and I wouldn't have it any other way. We're so blessed that she helps us clean up all the crayons and crumbs without complaining. What drives her is her love for God, and she knows that "God cleans up our messes."

I also dedicate this book to all the parents who could just use a break—not another Bible study to attend, but a *real* break.

On the night I started to write this book, my two-year-old was lying in my bed, refusing sleep. I thought I'd finally have time to myself to read the Bible and pray, like I want to or I feel I need to. But my child is here. Snuggling up to me and trying to touch the computer. I'm very grateful I have him, but let's get real for a second—I could use a break. And I'm sure you could, too.

Contents

Introduction

I'm a mother of four amazingly wonderful, busy, chatty, playful, unique, loud, and hungry children, currently ages two, four, six, and ten. I also have three children in heaven. I prayed and believed God to have these children. I'm forever grateful for the Word of God and for the faith that trials and tribulations in my life has produced. I had to persevere and choose to believe God and not listen to all the negativity surrounding my circumstances. And when our faith baby was born, we felt unstoppable.

A testimony like this may sound wonderful, and you might assume I reflect upon it every day and see my children as those amazing faith babies, but I don't. That's the truth.

I remind myself that while Jesus' mother, Mary, gave birth to Him—the King of Kings—she still had to feed Him, clothe Him, soothe Him, and take care of Him to the best that she knew how.

I often wish to be a much better mom than I am. I wish I could do a lot more for my children than I do. I wish I could cook better food for them. I wish they'd never cry or get hurt. I wish I didn't get angry or raise my voice or say things I shouldn't say. Yet I must remind myself is that I'm trying my best, like Mary did.

God didn't tell us how to do all things the right way, or the one and only way to do them; He just asks us to listen to Him daily and He'll show us the way.

As of the writing of this book, my husband and I have been pastoring our own church for more than five years. The same simple faith that turned our family around, turned our whole lives around. We began to believe God for every area of our lives and see the promises in His Word to claim as our own promises. Faith isn't complicated—God calls us to just believe and walk. As we continue to do that, we've been able to see so many other people start to live in this freedom, as well. Testimonies after testimonies will keep you encouraged—even on a tough day.

I'm at a point in my life when so many things are happening, and it's all very exciting, but it's a difficult balancing act with all the balls I'm juggling in the air. I feel like I'm running on a hamster wheel every day, and I barely get a chance to stop and drink a little water. From the moment my alarm (or child) wakes me up, I never seem to stop working until I hit the pillow at night—my own pillow, not one of my children's, since their bed is also my other bed.

I miss the routines I used to have. I miss my freedom. I would like to take care of myself more, but sometimes I just feel too tired.

Yet I feel like there are too many ways we as parents can get down on ourselves, especially in the church. You might think no one understands all that you're going through and feeling. You might feel like you carry the weight of the world on your shoulders, and just when you think you're starting to master the routines at home, you find yourself spiritually flat. Then condemnation tries to creep in, and out comes the measuring stick we use against ourselves, other parents, and those in the church and ministry.

The road is slippery, and it's all too well travelled.

What I have come to learn in this journey so far is that each parent can relate to another. And we can be filled up daily from God, even when we don't read or pray or do everything that "all the other Christians" might be doing.

We need God and we need each other—and maybe someone else to help pick up the crayons and sweep up the crumbs.

chapter one

Daily Routine

SOME PEOPLE DON'T THINK THEY HAVE A DAILY ROUTINE, BUT subconsciously, we all do. It could be very simple, but it's still there. If you were to just get dressed and go to work every day, that's still a routine. Let's face it—if you did those two things in the wrong order, there would certainly be an issue.

When I didn't have children, I had plenty of time for me. Even when I got married, I still had my own space to be me, to create, to think, to work, to simply refresh and rejuvenate. I had time to wake up in the morning and read the Bible, starting my day off with prayer and praise. My husband and I had time to attend not only conferences (together) but also regular Bible studies. We even had time to start and run our own ministries and enjoy the freedom of making our own schedules. We could go out for dinner regularly and eat whatever we wanted. We had time to focus on our marriage and relationship.

Then we decided to have a baby, having no idea what that all entailed. But we loved each other, and we believed a baby would multiply all that love.

After our first child, we tried hard to do all the things we use to do, and keep our same routines. I thought we could handle anything that new bundle of joy would bring. That's not exactly how it went down.

For a long time, we brought our son everywhere we went, and he became a part of everything in which we were involved. Exhausted, yet making ourselves look like we were still all put together, we fought hard to keep up with the image of other families. What we didn't realize is that at church, at special events, in photographs, on Facebook, on Instagram, etc., we only saw the good parts of other parents and families.

Our firstborn, Daniel, was what some might call a "good baby." He didn't fuss much and we could take him out to a lot of places. However, he also didn't want to leave my side. He couldn't have any sleepovers with any of his grandparents; he just wanted his mom. I certainly didn't mind all this love he was pouring out on me, but it became very tiring at times. I was determined to read books and get advice on parenting. There had to be some secrets that I just wasn't aware of.

As a family, we had to learn how to do things differently from what we had done before children. Trust me, it takes a lot of effort to plan and prioritize your family. This isn't something that'll just happen one day; you physically have to put yourself to work.

Daniel had his own schedule, and if we didn't follow it or pay attention to the cues he was giving us, everyone could get plenty frustrated, and we didn't want to live that way—feeling exhausted and frustrated. We also desired to focus on God together as a family and had to adjust our routines so we could do just that.

Our priorities changed and we had a new game plan. Our daily routine had to include our son's routine, and when we were able to include that, life became much easier.

I can't tell you what your game plan is for this time in your life, but I can tell you that it's okay to adjust and keep adjusting. This is your family, and the decisions you make for them are most important and pleasing to God. He's the one who created you and has the best for you; He wants you to enjoy every season of your life.

We decided to hold on to only a few ministry responsibilities and let go of some that we couldn't focus on much anymore. Our sleep pattern had to change. If I wanted to function properly, I needed to be able to sleep when our baby went to bed. We ensured we also didn't stay out late with him at every function.

When you make decisions like these, not everyone is going to agree or like them, but that doesn't matter. You need to make the decisions for your family because you'll need to live with them.

More Children

After the birth of our second child, I was very blessed to be able to stay at home with our children. With my husband pastoring and us having our own sports leagues business, I could do a lot of our paperwork and organizing from home. We also had just sold our home and moved in with my parents at this time; it was a full house, but great to have them so close by. Soon we were able to purchase our family home from them, and after a little while (probably once we got the hang of things with two kids in tow), my parents moved out.

As this routine got well underway, we surely thought we were doing okay. Yes, life with two boys was fun, and because of their age difference—three-and-a-half years—they got along well. Daniel was ready to go to preschool, but my husband and I weren't quite sure what the best choice was for him at this point. Of course, many children go to preschool, but because I was able to stay at home, we waited until he was old enough to go to part-time kindergarten to send him to school. But every child is different, and when our second son, Dominic, was old enough to go to preschool, we did send him. He was extremely energetic and enthusiastic about school, and had stopped napping as soon as he turned three.

Having one child was definitely life-changing and a whole routine changer, while having two felt very normal and complete. *We can do this; we're experts now,* we'd think. But then we added more children to our crew. I once heard a comedian say that having three kids feels like you're drowning, and having four feels like you're drowning *and* someone throws you a baby. Yes, I can certainly relate to that statement.

I'm pretty sure that for the next six years of my life, I blinked, and it just flew by. I'm amazed at some of the events that have occurred, the babies born, the house moves, the ministry and business growth, not to mention the many birthday parties, school concerts, lost teeth, and potty training. Did I mention I have three boys and one girl? Oh, the wrestling matches and the princess drama around the house can be very entertaining—or just downright insane.

With four children, my own routine was constantly changing. It felt like nothing was ever stable, and as soon as everything seemed to be functioning smoothly, it was a holiday, time change, or even summer vacation again, which would inevitably throw everything off. All our hard work in creating routines, or peace and tranquility in the home, was ruined. Time to adjust—*again.*

It's hard not to put everyone and everything else in front of your own needs; however, it's not always necessary. As a mother, I find it comes naturally for me to make sure our house is in order, bills are paid, groceries are bought, laundry is done, children are fed and clothed, and then—and only then—can I sit down and have a moment to myself.

This has become the toughest struggle for me. I want all these things done, and done well, and if they're not up to my standards, I can get so down on myself. But I have learned one thing: How can I put my best foot forward if I don't even know what my feet look like anymore? Time to break my routine and paint my toenails.

The routine I'd like to have right now in my devotion life is not the routine I'm keeping. My children mostly sleep through the night now, but I still can't manage to wake myself any earlier to read and pray before the world wakes up and puts demands on me. After I'm finished making breakfast, packing lunches, getting the children dressed, with hair and teeth brushed, signing their homework, and getting them out the door, I sit with my two-year-old to eat the leftover breakfast and drink cold coffee. I'm glad that my youngest loves worship music (most of the time), and I can fill my Spirit up with that during those moments.

My routine has felt so messy, but I realize it's still productive. I've been growing my faith the way God is leading me to. I don't need to feel bad about missing out on church events or conferences, or measuring my Christian growth with how many chapters in the Bible I'm reading. I know God can meet me where I am, and if I'm willing to open myself to new ways of growing my faith, then He'll show me.

Not long ago, I desired to pray in the Spirit more than I had been doing. I asked God to remind me daily and make me more sensitive to it. I soon found myself washing dishes while praying in tongues, driving while praying in tongues, showering while praying in tongues, etc. I realized that although I had thought it was a good idea to wake up early and pray in the Spirit, it wasn't always possible for me to do so, and I didn't need to feel bad about it. I could incorporate prayer in the Spirit into my everyday life.

I know God can meet me where I am, and if I'm willing to open myself to new ways of growing my faith, then He'll show me.

Some nights, when I was able to get the kids to bed early, I'd get excited to have my own quiet time if my husband was out playing basketball, or, if he was home, enjoy prayer time together. But if my expectations weren't met, I'd get quite disappointed. It seemed like whenever those opportunities opened up, they'd quickly get messed up—for example, a child would wake up and want me in their bed.

But the night that I'd asked God for more opportunity to pray in the Spirit, while lying in my child's bed, He revealed to me that I could pray quietly in tongues during regular activities; in fact, I began to feel the Holy Spirit's prompting so heavy at those times. No longer did I feel as though I had to wait for quiet time, for the "right" time; no longer was I getting frustrated in the day or night about these missed opportunities, because I realized I had so many opportunities to talk to God and pray. I know that my prayers move mountains—no matter where or how I prayed.

> *Jesus says, "'Truly I tell you, if anyone says to this mountain, "Go, throw yourself into the sea," and does not doubt in their heart but believes that what they say will happen, it will be done for them.'"*
>
> —Mark 11:23–24

Reality

I'm glad we don't have a dishwasher. God speaks to me when I'm doing the dishes. He also speaks to me when I'm cleaning the house. There's fulfillment in making things clean and putting my house in order, but maybe it's also become therapeutic. God often gives me new ideas and messages to share as I'm cleaning up. This is where the crayons and crumbs come in; I wouldn't have them or be constantly cleaning them if I didn't have my children, for whom I'm very grateful.

Unfortunately, for the past ten years now, I haven't caught up on my sleep. I hear everything that happens in the night and I'm always ready to spring into action. But God's grace is sufficient for me, and He will still speak and work through me, even when I'm physically weak. He gives us everything we need when we need it.

Spiritually, physically, and financially, God provides for all my needs and continually desires to work anew in my life. I just need to talk to Him; He will speak to me and guide me.

It's okay for God to break my routine—He needs to. I'm happier when He does, and so is my family!

chapter two

Adding More to Your Plate

I HAVE LEARNED THAT YOU SHOULD ALWAYS ACT NOW HOW YOU WOULD need to act if you were to double the size or capacity—at least that's what my husband and I have learned for our business. You should have the right plans and procedures in place now so that when there's growth, you're not scrambling last minute.

This may be wise business advice, but it can absolutely be applied to parenting, as well. While having one child dramatically changes everything in your life, having more will only add to your plate—both the blessings and the stress. If you can create some great routines and life hacks of your own when you have one child, then you'll be more confident when more children come along.

Looking back, I know that whether you have one child or desire a child, your mind drastically changes. I remember making that decision to start a family, and that required new thinking. It required preparation. Like many things in life, we must prepare beforehand. With children, it seems one can never prepare enough. Each child is different and so is each family. You might (and should) make plans, but let God be the one to direct your steps. *"Many are the plans in a person's heart, but it is the Lord's purpose that prevails"* (Proverbs 19:21).

After you do some internal changes of your own, and then an amazing bundle of joy comes into your life, that's when you find out what you're really made of.

I tried to listen to what a lot of great women told me about being a mom and taking care of my baby (and myself), but I wasn't those women. Their children were not mine. Not everything that worked for them worked for me, and why should it? I'm me. You've probably seen how you think parenting should look. You see things in your own family growing up that you either like or don't like. You see things in other parents that you like or don't like. Then you try to form your own plan of action, because you seriously need one.

I love my husband to pieces, but he tends to panic first and then implement some sort of solution. I plan ahead. I think it's because I was the one awake at all hours of the night with a newborn, giving me plenty of time to think and sometimes cry out to God for help.

My body was shocked that it couldn't get a good night's sleep anymore. Physically, I was exhausted, and it was time to figure out some sort of plan to help me not lose my cool. I realized that it *does* take a village to raise a child. I appreciated the help of others and began to understand the importance of rest when I could and taking a walk when possible. I love to walk outside and clear my head. I knew that having that head space away from the baby was crucial, although not always possible. There have been times when I was stuck in the house for days on end—not because I didn't have any help, but because I wanted everything done a certain way.

There was plenty that I, a new mom, had to learn, and it didn't always have to do with my baby, but myself. Having this amazing little miracle affected every area of my life. I had to learn how to be a better me. I couldn't clean the house, or even myself, like I wanted to, which made me feel like I was failing. Other moms seemed to keep their houses clean, prepare healthy food, and put their makeup on (or so I thought). Why couldn't I?

I could barely get out of my pajamas, wash my hair, eat a whole meal, or clean up all the baby's bottles by the time my husband got home for dinner. Sundays were a huge challenge for us all to get a good night's sleep the night before, get dressed, and eat before heading to church, where we put a smile on our faces and showed everyone just how "put together" we were. As the saying goes, the struggle is real.

Finally, one day, I caught a vision. From praying to God in my desperation and reaching my limits emotionally, I found and purchased a baby sleep book. I was sure it would have the information I needed. If I could just get a better night's sleep and eat properly, I knew I'd be able to function better. If I couldn't, I would suffer, but so would my baby.

I found the challenge of making a routine work for both the baby and me, which meant I could put my own well-being first, which would ultimately benefit us both. When I was able to take care of myself, I was able to take care of him, and enjoy it, too. It turned out to be a helpful book, and it didn't take too much trial and error to come up with our own sleeping habits and—eventually—a full night's sleep for all of us.

Now, in the waking hours, I also needed to give us a plan to follow. I knew eating and exercising properly would benefit me and give me the strength I needed, and help me feel good about myself, too. I had to decide to put the baby down in his chair or crib so I could make myself a meal. Hearing him cry wasn't easy, but I knew he was safe. It sometimes felt unnecessary to leave the baby with his dad or grandparents, just to go for a walk by myself at the end of the day, but alone time was (and is) so important. I needed to clear my head and enjoy the peace God wanted to share with me.

Although my sweet firstborn son didn't like to stay with his dad or grandparents at first, looking for me instead, I stuck to my decision and walked away. The funny thing is that when I did leave to go for a walk, he was unhappy at first, but that quickly changed and he began to enjoy the time with everyone else. My baby learned to adjust and connect with the rest of his family. I had to learn to trust God in this area and to trust others with my baby.

Learning to put us all on a plan when we had one baby was very beneficial to everyone. During the times that were not quite so planned, we were able to enjoy each other and life more because we were all at ease. Even when others watched the baby, I quickly accepted the fact that they're not me and will do things a little differently, things that could mess up our routines a bit. But even when routines became messy, it wouldn't take too long to get them back again because this plan had become something the baby and our family were used to; it was our way of life.

When more babies joined our family, we had proof that our plan had worked once and so we implemented the same ideas and routines. There were definitely challenges—new ones. We had to fit a toddler and a new baby into the same plans, but when they didn't work as we expected, we eventually made new ones.

Our sleep and nap times had to work out for two children now—never mind an exhausted mom (and tired dad). Cooking for the toddler, cooking for myself, and breastfeeding was all a bit too much to handle in an orderly fashion. People complimented me on losing weight so quickly after our second baby, but honestly? The weight probably dropped because I wasn't feeding myself properly. Eventually, we did get the hang of things and felt like we were in control again. Our family was growing and changing, so our ways of working everything out had to change, as well.

When we added another two children to our family, bringing the total to four, the house—and our schedule—became full. At this point in our lives, two were in school full time, one part time, and the youngest still at home (but eagerly anticipating school). We sometimes forgot to pick them up for early dismissal, to pack all the right clothing or food, and even to take one home from school, but every day is new—"We got this!" we'd remind ourselves.

We've heard some great advice over the years, but implementing anything new in your life will look differently from other families' plans. We see the changes in our children when they go to bed earlier, eat better, and are engaged in an activity. These are good things for our kids to do, but even good things can become boring and mundane. Even though we had a good underlying plan in place, it only manifested some of the time.

Nighttime for the school-aged children had involved a routine of dinner, homework, and bedtime by 8 p.m. If they desired to participate in any school sports, then it had to be something that worked well for the whole family. While they're currently in the same elementary school, this seems to be working. I'm not sure what this will look like next year when all the children are in school, but I try not to worry about that.

Dinner and evening snacks make it into our routine, too. If they like what I've prepared for them, then I've done great. After school, the kids always seem to be hungry, so if there are any immediate sports or activities, we need snacks—*lots* of snacks. Even picking up a hamburger or chicken nuggets can help when we're in a pinch, so if the budget allows, that's what we do. (Tip: The greatest trick I've figured out so far is that if I only bring vegetables or "boring" healthy food, the kids will actually eat it because they're "starving.")

But then, after-school snacks or even early dinner comes with a price: hungry children right before bed. Now, I ensure there's something the kids can nibble on before bed; they *never* let me forget. And even if they haven't eaten that dreaded banana that's still in their lunch bag, they'll eat that before bed if they're hungry enough.

Trying to hit all the major food groups is a constant job—both for my children and me. At least if I'm putting in the effort, I will have victory every now and then.

On a regular weeknight, by the time an activity is over, dinner is eaten, homework is done, and snack is eaten, it's already 7:30 p.m. and it's time to get ready for bed. Then there's still a bath or shower, plus devotion and prayer time, *then* bedtime—finally.

When others witness our routine, it may seem rigid, or even unnecessary, to them and they might wonder why we do what we do—but it works for our kids, for our family. When our children get to bed early, they usually are happier in the morning. I like to see them happy and well rested; it makes all our days more enjoyable.

"Therefore do not worry about tomorrow, for tomorrow will worry about itself. Each day has enough trouble of its own" (Matthew 6:34).

I must focus on one day at a time.

God can still speak and move freely in all this craziness of planning and preparation. That may seem contradictory, but when we're all "prepared," it eases our minds. When I have a plan in place, I don't need to think about what my next steps are; I can freely move and think about other things. I'll be able to hear God through it all. I know that plans can totally get messed up, but if they do, I have already been in a place of peace; therefore, I'm able to make better decisions.

GOD CAN STILL SPEAK AND MOVE FREELY IN ALL THIS CRAZINESS OF PLANNING AND PREPARATION.

> *Great peace have those who love your law, and nothing can make them stumble.*
>
> —Psalm 119:165

chapter three

Dealing with Demands

If I were to listen to everything my family, my church leaders, and society said to me about my life and how everything should be, I'd be a total mess.

What people around us suggest isn't necessarily wrong; in fact, they could be offering good advice, but just because it works for them, doesn't mean it works for everyone. If I were to listen to and act on every piece of advice, then I'd be so far from who I am as a person, and who God is to me, that I would be headed for destruction.

That's something parents don't often realize they're doing to themselves until it's too late, and sickness, depression, or anxiety creeps in. We can put some unfair demands on ourselves and think that they're positive because others have told us so. What you must realize is that advice comes from someone who has found success in an area in their lives—*their* lives, not *yours*. It might not work for you. I want to emphasize this to you because I want you to know that it's okay if you can't implement something that you have been told or shown.

Any change in your life brings about decisions that could make you look like you need help or you're unstable. Change is good and is always happening. But for onlookers (everyone else), they might feel the need to help you in some way. This is good, and it does show they care.

For example, perhaps your family is offering support and help. Their advice might be very beneficial to you. They might see some things that you don't or understand you more than a friend does. Sometimes what they say hurts, because they know you better than others. But just because they know you the best, doesn't always mean what they say is what you need to do or implement. You need to know *you!*

We often put unrealistic demands on ourselves—especially during holiday seasons. At family get-togethers, perhaps where you haven't seen family in a while, relatives have plenty of things to say about how you look, how your children are acting, etc., and throw out so many questions you find yourself stumbling over the answers. You try to read their expressions to see whether you've "passed the test." This happened to me regularly; I left family functions and celebrations feeling like I was just never going to measure up. These were the demands I put on myself. But I didn't have to take everything so personally and hold on to it.

I think it's hard not to take these things to heart, though, because family is supposed to be the closest to you, so everything they do and say can hit you deeply. And if you're already feeling like you're failing in some areas, it can be disheartening to hear any more negative words spoken.

We—parents, mothers, fathers, and all humans—need encouragement always, especially when it looks like we have it all together. I know I've put on a fake smile when I didn't feel like smiling. Maybe it wasn't always fake, though, as it was also good practice of what I *wanted* to be like. But then after the holidays, I'd go home and wonder what they would think of me, running around the house yelling at my children, laundry everywhere and dinners not made.

If I could've just encouraged myself and talked myself through the "why we do what we do," I could've enjoyed more moments throughout the hustle and bustle. What I've realized is that much of my family have great ideas and advice because they've been through the tender stages of parenthood, but I had never seen them going through them. When we endure hardships, we tend to hide instead of asking for help or encouragement. I believe that if we were all more open about our struggles and the steps we took to overcome them, we would be able to help many more people; this is especially true in our own families.

Another significant part of my life has been my church and ministry. Church could be an amazing, encouraging place to be, but it was up to me to make it that way; I couldn't put that responsibility on others. Church was another place where I had to interact with many people who knew who I was and could see how things were going on the outside. The smiles I gave through tired eyes and with crying children in tow were giveaways that things weren't perfect. Many people assume that being a pastor's wife equals a perfect life—a husband who's always praying for me and our children, and who would know exactly what to do or say to his amazing wife—but that was simply not the case.

At home, our faith was being stretched and we had to learn how to be better in every area of our lives so that we could make the best possible life for us and our children. I wanted to be happy and give the impression that I truly was, but it was a struggle. As pastors, we encourage everyone to get involved and stay involved at church. People need encouragement and to live a life around faith-filled believers. My husband and I encourage everyone to grow their faith and stay connected with God daily. But I know as a mom, and someone who can put so much pressure on myself, that this can just add to the overwhelming schedule I already have.

I was responsible for running many of the church's programs, and even with juggling my four children's schedules, it did look easier for me to do it because our family was already at the church much of the time; we pastored it. For us, there are things we can do, so we do them—being at the church together as a family is our priority. But we also knew how to make it fun and enjoyable, and get help when we needed it.

I think that when our family makes church an option and attends only when the circumstances are aligned, then we'll miss out on all the encouragement and blessings from our Father that we need. He wants our family to be in a church family that are His hands and feet, those who will stand beside us and encourage us in every season of our lives.

No one is perfect, and no church is, either, but when there's something that you think your church needs or should do—maybe *you* are that person to do it.

When I was in college, I attended a major youth event the college hosted, and at the end of the night, I noticed my coat was missing; someone had taken it. It was a Christian college, and I hung my coat in nearly the same spot every day, and it was gone. Instead of letting this annoyance fester, I decided to get positively proactive. So, the next year when this event came around again, I decided to help out and organize a coat check. It required effort, planning, and time, but in the end, I helped a lot of people enjoy themselves at the event while feeling secure.

I have carried that same thought process into every area of my life. God is always walking us through all sorts of situations and we have the opportunity to learn or complain. When we learn, we open bigger doors of opportunity; however, when we complain, we shut God out. We can't hear Him when we're only listening to ourselves complain.

God has placed each of us where we are for a reason. We can look around and take opportunities to make things better or worse. In our families, workplaces, communities, and churches, we're faced with decisions every day to be a light in this world (or not).

God has placed each of us where we are for a reason. We can look around and take opportunities to make things better or worse.

When I sit and look at my own situation, my vision can be so narrow. It's so important that I stay tuned in to what God wants to say through it all. I don't believe a lot of what I see in the news, on TV, or Facebook, and that's why I can't spend my valuable time on these outlets. My world around me and the view I have of it comes from the Bible and what God is telling me through His Word. I could read it a hundred times and get a hundred new revelations from it. Every time I'm connected with God, I'm growing.

You'll always have situations or feelings that will try to trip you up some days, but know that you're God's child and He has a great life for you. He wants to lift you up every day and make it better than the day before.

Moms, parents, caregivers, I pray you receive the encouragement you need daily and that you'll encourage others, too. I pray you'll set your own standards and not be too hard on yourself. I pray you'll look around this world that you're living in and see all the opportunities, beauty, and blessings that your heavenly Father has given you. And I pray you'll enjoy every moment.

chapter four

Keeping the Balance

God, marriage, family, work, ministry, friends, vacations, shopping—organizing it all can seem impossible when I try to balance my life. I try to correct the out-of-balance part a lot, and I only know it's out of balance when the scale tips over.

It always feels like work to try to balance the scale, but perhaps if I didn't work at it, then I wouldn't see the rewards. We can have a lot going on in our lives all at once, and that can cause us to crash if the weight isn't balanced out. A girlfriend of mine was so thin that when she was pregnant, she literally tipped over. I was a bit jealous because I felt as big as a house every time I was pregnant, but then again, I could stand up somewhat normally. The weight (in this case, literally) was balanced.

You need to give yourself a pat on the back for even trying to make a schedule. Getting out the agenda, the notebook, or cell phone and sitting down to plan things out is a step in the right direction. When you can complete even the most menial task, it's an accomplishment that boosts your confidence and self-esteem.

So, time to get working. I'm someone who loves to make lists; maybe you're like me, or maybe you hate list-making, but either way, how many times do parents forget the list or have to write out a new one on the go?

Let's face it, life can just get hectic, and forgetting things to do or get done doesn't help the organizational process. It's important to remind yourself why you do what you do. When you're better organized, it will make you feel better and therefore you will enjoy these times in your life—not to mention that those around you will benefit from your organization and better attitude. For myself, I notice how happier I am when I feel like I'm accomplishing something. I found that strapping a baby to me and vacuuming the house turned out to be very enjoyable. Baby fell asleep and I had a clean floor; even if it only lasted a little while, it was still worth it.

When the babies were little, I went through a season when I felt completely overwhelmed when I thought of trying to get organized. But if I didn't take time to make the littlest shopping list for my husband, then I'd definitely run out of a lot of important items. Sometimes even just getting the laundry done seemed like a daunting task. I have pictures of my youngest son sleeping in the laundry hamper on the floor; I was multitasking.

No matter your children's age, it's important you're able to see where there needs to be balance in your life. I find that now that most of my children are in school, I prefer to work all our family times around the school schedule. However, we can get into such a crazy school and homework routine that we just need to break it up sometimes. For example, we've taken the opportunity to take the kids out of school early or even miss a day or two because we need a family break or vacation. Our weekends are so busy with church that we don't often get to go away for the weekend, so we must make our own schedule. It often works out quite well.

Peace in our homes and our lives is what we all want, and when we can prioritize our priorities, then I do believe we can have a home and a life full of peace. Ultimately, everyone wants to live a peaceful, stress-free life. It doesn't mean that you never leave your house or never see any kind of conflict, but it does mean that you can live in such a worry-free state of mind. When we put God and His Word first, then our relationship with Him becomes top priority. It should be top priority because we will be better at being whom He created us to be when we're connected first to our Creator.

When I'm filled by God, then I can better give of myself in my marriage and then to my children. I can create a peaceful home. I can create the atmosphere of peace and joy. When our priorities get out of balance is when we see it cause breakdown in our home and family.

Our attitudes play a lot into how we feel and affect the atmosphere around us and how others feel. When our home takes a turn for the worse and the "grumps" start flying all over the place, it's important to take a stand and make a change.

Sometimes I literally sit down and wonder who brought in the grumpy attitudes and negativity, because it does come in from somewhere and is then passed around. It can start from the tiniest complaint or negative feeling, or reflect stress in the workplace or other situations in which we're involved throughout the day. But when we continue to dwell on situations or other people, then we give those situations and people priority in our minds—rather than peace and happiness—and our balance does, well, tip.

When you think about your life changing and beginning a new season, this is a fantastic opportunity to get yourself organized and determined to make some changes. It's important to have a vision for what this new season will look like. Write down the goals and dreams you have for your family, your business, your health, etc., for this new season that you're in. *"'For I know the plans I have for you,' declares the Lord, 'plans to prosper you and not to harm you, plans to give you hope and a future'"* (Jeremiah 29:11). If God has a wonderful plan for us, and says He gives us the desires of our heart (Psalm 37:4), then why are we not dreaming big?

> WHEN YOU THINK ABOUT YOUR LIFE CHANGING AND BEGINNING A NEW SEASON, THIS IS A FANTASTIC OPPORTUNITY TO GET YOURSELF ORGANIZED AND DETERMINED TO MAKE SOME CHANGES.

I encourage you to write down everything you desire, everything you'd like to do and be, and keep the list with you. Never shy away or look at your list in a negative way. Your God created you unique and you must rise up because you live in victory daily; even if you don't believe that yet, choose to believe it. God loves you so much and His promises are for you today in every one of your circumstances.

What's it going to take for you to achieve some of the things on your list? Take your list and pray over it, asking God to give you the ideas to get the ball rolling.

chapter five

I Need a Break

"I NEED A BREAK." I'VE FOUND THIS IS SOMETHING I'VE WANTED TO SAY *a lot.* I need a break. I could use a break. I'd love a break. Mommy needs some alone time. Mommy could use some help.

What I've realized is that although I found myself saying—or thinking—these things, I wasn't sure what a "break" actually meant. I couldn't tell you what kind of break I needed or what a break looked like. Saying the words just meant I had hit some sort of limit in the natural and that I needed a change.

I needed a change that would give me some sort of relief—in my mind, in my emotions, or even in my body. I was exhausted and looking for ways to relieve the stress I'd created. Yes, these wonderful children, and my situation, were things I'd chosen to create. I love my children like crazy, but sometimes I feel like *I'm* the crazy one trying to hold their whole universe together.

Where and how we live stems from all the choices we've made. How our lives function and the routines we take on come from our choices. As parents, we often put so much pressure on ourselves that we can sometimes feel like giving up. That's another way to express that we just need a break. It's okay to feel this way, as it happens to all of us. But then what?

What do you do when your home life is crazy, your social life is nonexistent, and you feel totally disconnected from society?

My advice? Invest in *you.*

Talk to God and tell Him what you need; He's always with you and ready to help.

I love the story in the Bible in which Mary, Jesus' mother, left Jesus at the temple and for three days didn't even notice he was gone (Luke 2:43–46). That must have been a tough realization. My stomach sinks when I try to put myself in her shoes. That was the Son of God, never mind her own son.

I feel better about my own circumstances when I think of this story. Their family must have been like ours—a little messy at times.

I need God to show me how to be the best mother I can be. I need Him to give me ideas, to help me teach my children and show my love for them. These things don't come naturally because humanity is sinful. But if I truly believe that God is moving and working in me, I can have the confidence to keep pressing on.

> *. . . being confident of this, that he who began a good work in you will carry it on to completion until the day of Christ Jesus.*
>
> —Philippians 1:6

God has a plan and purpose for my future (Jeremiah 29:11). He also said He gives me the desires of my heart (Psalm 37:4), and I desire to have supernatural help from God for parenting.

A break for me means needing a new solution to my current situation.

Sometimes I need to have a nap. Parenting comes with sleep deprivation, period. It's hard to function at your best when you're lacking quality sleep—restful, deep, and undisturbed. I could use a longer sleep at night or a nap during the day when I'm not worried about cooking, laundry, paying bills, or thinking about the kids and our ministry.

> A BREAK FOR ME MEANS NEEDING A NEW SOLUTION TO MY CURRENT SITUATION.

Sometimes I need to have a shower. My alone time in the washroom is precious. I feel like there are a million eyes on me when I need to go to the washroom. I've found myself having to hide or explain my body parts and functions to little people with many questions.

When the babies were little, they didn't have questions, although I had to bring them in there with me. But when they were toddlers, I wanted to lock the door, but then I'd be tormented with thoughts of what these children were capable of doing out of my sight. Sometimes I found my daughter standing on our dining room table trying to grab the chandelier, and my son sitting on top of the fridge. I know they're mischievous and very smart. Taking the time to simply wash my hair and shave can absolutely take away all my feelings of frustration and failure, leaving me torn.

Sometimes a break means leaving the kids and getting out of the house. Although I often haven't known where to go, and I didn't want to go alone, simply going for a walk was a nice option—just me, Jesus, and the great outdoors. My brain enjoyed some quiet time while the fresh air was very good for me.

My husband often suggested I sign up for a gym membership, but I'd laugh. Working out *and* committing to yet another thing was the furthest from my mind. God bless him, he tried, and I love him.

However, all these options made *me* the focus, which was a struggle. But I saw that I needed to invest some time in myself. It was where the balance was toppling over; I wasn't taking care of myself properly and needed some "me time."

Grandparents, other relatives, neighbours, and babysitters are necessary, too. My husband and I know we need to prioritize a break together. From going out for a meal to eventually going away for the night was a major, welcoming break. That precious time has helped to refocus our family life and vision. We can take time to plan for our life and family during our break, and eat at any restaurant we chose. "Table for two" is very cozy!

Being able to do household tasks and grocery shopping without the children around was even a blessing. Walking the store aisles and holding hands is a small thing we can do, but a very meaningful one. Simple love language and opportunity yield great rewards.

While your babies are little, life can feel like it's passing you by. But you're doing the most important thing you could be doing—taking care of that baby and those children the best you can. It can be exhausting, I know, but that's a good time to pray and ask God to bring you the help you need. Sometimes, it can just be new ideas and ways of learning how you can parent; other times, help can come from moments of silence and rest for your body. When you can make a choice to praise God through it all, you can enjoy some wonderful moments.

This has happened a few times in my life now; one, two, or even three of my kids are crying at the same time and suddenly I'm laughing. I want to cry along with them, but I find myself in a hysterical laughter I can't contain; sure enough, all my children start laughing, too. I know those must be "God" moments; He saw the help I needed.

One of the most tiring—and precious—moments I've ever experienced was the very long night during which my toddler decided that he just wasn't going to sleep. He came to my room, woke me up, and told me to come to his bed. But he didn't want to cuddle and sleep; he wanted to talk. I finally coaxed him to close his eyes, and I guess I did, too. Suddenly, he was crawling over me to get out of bed. I woke up and assumed he needed to use the washroom or get a drink of water or something, but no, he was just restless. We went back to his bed, snuggled, and slept for about an hour.

Then he woke again, up and moving around. This time, I heard him walk to our back stairs. Since his grandparents lived in the basement, and it was only an hour or so before we all had to get up, I let him walk down the stairs. My mother always heard his little feet coming down the stairs and would run to him, so I fell back asleep.

In a little while, I could hear him in the hallway outside his bedroom door. Had he not gone downstairs? I felt terrible now—terribly tired but also almost sick to my stomach because I hadn't followed him downstairs to make sure he was all right. I quickly bounced out of his bed and called for him. He came into his bedroom and hopped back on his bed. I asked him if he was okay and what he was doing in the hallway.

"I was playing with Jesus," he explained simply.

"What?" I replied.

"We played rock-paper-scissors," he went on.

I smiled tiredly. "Oh, you mean you were playing rock-paper-scissors with *Papa*?"

"Nope," he insisted. "I was playing with Jesus." So I asked him what he looked like. "He has hair like Grandma."

Wow! My son talked about that experience for weeks. I pray he'll always remember that; I know I will.

> *But he said to me, "My grace is sufficient for you, for my power is made perfect in weakness." Therefore I will boast all the more gladly about my weaknesses, so that Christ's power may rest on me.*
>
> —2 Corinthians 12:9

That night, I felt very weak, and my judgment was poor, but my God is greater.

Thank You, Jesus!

chapter six

Every Day Is a Gift

I NEVER WANT TO STAY IN THE PLACE OF GRUMBLING OR COMPLAINING, even though that's an ongoing challenge in my current everyday life. I get tired of cleaning up crumbs, spilled milk, dirty clothes, throw-up, or worse. I get frustrated stepping on crayons and breaking them. I can't count the times I've banged my head on the boys' bunk-bed, banged my shin on a bike pedal, or tripped over yet another toy.

Parenting can be so dangerous. It can be so unnerving, complicated, and just flat-out tiring. Yet what a great workout it can be! Chasing the children, climbing stairs, pretending to be a pony or a rocket ship, lifting, carrying, and dragging them and *all* their many toys around—who needs a gym membership? This is what brings the gray hairs and wrinkles... and the wonderful memories, too.

I realized that every day I'm given is a gift. Even if I don't feel like opening the gift until after I've had my coffee, it's still a gift, from God. What I do with that gift is up to me. Sometimes I catch myself staring at my children as they play and as their imagination takes them away. I like to see their eyes fill with awe and wonder of the things around them, things that I tend to think are basic, mundane, normal.

Yet they think of them as amazing and worth taking the time to explore. Walking down the sidewalk with them can take so long, especially when I'm in a hurry to get somewhere, because they need to touch or step in everything, but that just shows me how to slow down, enjoy the moment, and not let life pass me by.

Every day, we can learn something new and experience something different and wonderful in our lives. Every day, we can pray and ask God to teach us, trust Him to lead us, and let Him fill us up.

God is *only* good. According to John 10:10, it's Satan who comes to steal, kill, and destroy, but Christ has come to bring us life, and life to the fullest!

When you find yourself in that place of frustration, stress, complaining, anxiety, and even depression, there's a reason behind it. We tend to lead ourselves into the darkness. The choices we make produce a routine in our lives and an expected outcome. If you find yourself in a place and a state of mind that you don't like, then you need to take time and see where you could have made different, better choices. When you can start to pinpoint actions or attitudes that you don't like, then address them and pray over yourself; you'll see change.

Of course, it helps to have prayers from others—your spouse, family, friends—but often, it's just you, your child(ren), and God who are around in those trying moments. He's always there with you. Take every thought captive and pray; talk to God and give Him all your frustrations and burdens.

When I've prayed out of frustration or desperation, God gives me the wisdom and solutions I need. Just the other day, I found myself becoming frustrated when my daughter wasn't taking her ABCs seriously and I didn't know how to teach her other than repeating going through the pictures we were looking at. As I felt my mounting frustration, and self-condemnation for feeling that way, I prayed quickly and quietly.

God (I know it was Him and not my own thoughts) gave me a silly song to sing about the alphabet and the sounds each letter makes. That song turned our attitudes right around and helped my daughter learn the ABCs in an unconventional way—a God-given way!

We can turn each day around and make it great. Great for ourselves, and for our children.

Even when the bad days come, you can always see God working everything out for your good. Our youngest son was with us at the church one evening during a midweek service. I left him in a room with his siblings for a total of two minutes; while I gave a short testimony, he tripped and split his chin open. I heard the screams as I finished my encouragement to the group and I ran into the room. He was holding his chin, crying. His siblings said he was just walking and then fell; there was no horseplay at all. They didn't think it was too bad until I picked him up and under his chin revealed a deep cut that needed stitches. He would be the first of my children to require stitches.

We immediately drove him to the closest hospital and prayed over him the entire way. At the emergency room, the nurses temporarily taped up his chin at the desk and told us to grab a seat, where we waited for three hours. My heart hurt so bad; I hated that I couldn't help him and take away his pain. But in this packed emergency room, our sweet boy suddenly started singing worship music. And he wasn't very quiet about it. He was the only child in there, so he had everyone's attention. We didn't stop him at all; in fact, there were so many smiles we started to see around the room. God was at work!

Our little man fell asleep for the rest of the waiting. The getting-the-stitches part that followed was terrible; I cried right along with him.

As parents, we desperately desire to have our children be healthy, happy, and the greatest they can be in this life. We desire to be the best parents we can be, but that happens only when we actively make Christ the centre of our hearts and our families. If we remember that our relationship with God is number one, then everything else falls into place. We gain confidence when we take time to hear God, and we learn to speak His Word over our family and our daily lives.

> IF WE REMEMBER THAT OUR RELATIONSHIP WITH GOD IS NUMBER ONE, THEN EVERYTHING ELSE FALLS INTO PLACE.

Church can sometimes feel like an "event" we do on Sundays, a place to go for the family, and we hope the kids will stay in children's church or Sunday School this time so we can experience the filling of the Holy Spirit. And yet I find that the most peace I experience, and the place where I'm filled up the most, is at home when my children are around (as crazy as that may sound).

I realized that if I'm talking to God all throughout the day and trying to add teachings (to children or adults) into my day, then God will speak to me, too. Maybe it's because I'm in my safe, comfort zone at home, and I can rest and be myself since I've established some good routines with my children, that I can relax and hear God's voice.

Daily I need Christ to speak to me. But we need others' encouragement, as well. It might feel like we don't know what we're doing when we're parenting; some things seem like tests and trials. And while it's wonderful to receive support from other parents and hear what they do and what's worked for them, remember that your way, for your family, is better. Adapt advice and wisdom to your own family situation. One way is even better: God's way.

I love God, my husband, and my children so much, but that doesn't mean I do everything right or I'm happy all the time. I realize happiness is a choice. I need to choose to be happy and choose to smile, even when things spiral out of control.

Being confident of who you are is important. Working on and investing in yourself is the best thing you can do for yourself. What are the things you like to do? Do them! As a child of God, be confident in what God has done for you and has now equipped you with. This takes reminding yourself of what the Word of God says about you.

Know who you are and be confident with the decisions you make. Hold your head up and help others to do the same. We can all have victory in this area of our lives, but it's even better to have that circle of support, lifting each other up in support and love. It truly does take a village to raise a child. I appreciate my village.

chapter seven

My Heavenly Help

THE HOLY SPIRIT WAS SENT TO BE OUR COMFORTER. AS I'M RAISING children, I need a comforter. I need help and peace in small and big decisions. No two days are the same, and no two children are the same.

Just when we may think we have it all under control, that's when we lose control again. Children will respond well when we take time to get to know each one individually and not put them all into the same box. Literally—if I were to put two of my children inside an opened cardboard box, they would fight. However, if each were to get their own box, I'd see their creativity and imagination run wild, giving them excitement and confidence.

Each of my children reacts, cries, learns, and speaks differently from the others. They also like different games, hobbies, food, and people. Constant change can be tough on an organized, predictable rule follower like me. I'm a fun, loving, caring, and generally happy person. But somewhere in the years of motherhood, I feel like I've turned a bit, well, crazy. I can blame it on the lack of sleep, of proper food, of proper exercise, or even lack of help, but I know what I need is to be filled up from the inside by the Holy Spirit, because then what's inside will come out.

There was a time in my life when I was spiritually frustrated. I wasn't seeing the results of my faith manifesting into my home life. I felt like I'd hit a plateau. I couldn't take the time to read and pray like I'd wanted to. As I talked about earlier, I had to make my own decision on what prayer time was going to look like for me. It was okay that I wasn't kneeling by my bedside but instead sitting in a circle with my children, doing devotions with them and then praying, hoping they were listening. God blesses those times, too. He loves it when I spend time with Him; after all, He's the one who created these children who don't always listen to their mother very well—He understands.

One evening, during devotions, I was the only one home putting all the kids to bed. Sometimes, I dreaded this part of the day. My children can be a little frustrating when they don't want to go to bed, or brush their teeth, or take a bath, or they're whining because they're hungry again or need their fiftieth cup of water, which can then start a whole new set of nighttime problems.

That evening, we did devotions together and then I played a worship song, thinking that maybe this would be a great way to improve our routine. What I didn't expect was God to pour out in our worship. We were all singing together, and suddenly I couldn't hold back the tears of joy. My one son, who doesn't show his worshipful side very much, singing quietly with his eyes closed, was a beautiful sight to see.

Right then, God gave me vision, and I could see Jesus dancing in a circle, holding hands with my other children—the ones I lost on earth but have in heaven. When I told my children what I'd just seen, we were all in tears of joy. It was such a special confirmation of

God's love and Spirit poured out upon us. My two oldest children still talk about it today.

I realize that if I want to see and hear God in my life more, I need to be listening more closely to His Spirit. He has given me access to all the help I will ever need and that can only come through His Spirit. *"For anyone who speaks in a tongue does not speak to people but to God"* (I Corinthians 14:2). I speak, pray, sing to God in tongues because I know that my spirit is connecting with His, and He will show me the revelations and wisdom I need. If God has all the peace and wisdom I need daily, and knows the way for me to live, then I need to tune in.

Sometimes, I just walk around the house and I speak or sing in tongues. The funny thing is that my youngest son will hear me and try to imitate; little does he know that he, too, is tapping in to the Spirit of God.

If I'm connecting with my heavenly language, then I need to take time not only to pray, but also to listen. Now that I connect in the Spirit, I can expect God to bring new ideas and wisdom to me. He even shows me things prophetically, both for myself and others.

IF WE DESIRE TO GROW IN OUR SPIRITUAL WALK WITH GOD, WE CAN DO SO, RIGHT NOW, RIGHT WHERE WE ARE.

If we desire to grow in our spiritual walk with God, we can do so, right now, right where we are.

The Spirit of God lives inside of us. When I read God's Word, He speaks to me then, too. It doesn't take much time to read scripture, because there's no maximum or minimum required. There have been times when I try to read with all the kids around, and because they're playing by themselves, I can tune in to the Word instantly; other times, it's just a gong show.

But I don't have to get frustrated. When the house is loud, I sometimes add to the noise, walking around the living room reading out loud, louder and louder, only then to rise up in the confidence and passion that the Word of God brings. *"In the beginning was the Word, and the Word was with God, and the Word was God"* (John 1:1). The Word is power and contains power; it will change the atmosphere.

If I'm willing to listen, then God will speak. Time and again, it takes only one verse to jump out and touch my heart. If I meditate on this verse, God will continue to speak to me about it all day (or days) long. And that's okay. I don't need to follow my one-year-of-reading-the-Bible devotion plan if God wants to spend time teaching me something from a specific verse.

During those days that can seem so long and exhausting, I might not always know what to pray over myself or my situation, but I can always pray in tongues and know that God is working on my behalf. I'll even go as far to say that to keep my sanity, I pray in tongues a lot.

I desired, and continue to desire, to see great changes in my own attitude toward my children and myself. I want to be the woman whom God has created me to be right now—not something I can have only later. Even though I might not be able to put all the time and energy into my church ministry that I'd like to, my most important ministry is here at home. My children need to see Jesus every day. They need to know the love of the Father. And the biggest job I have is to usher in the presence of God into my home.

Sure, I might not always have a peaceful home, but that doesn't mean God isn't there. God waits patiently for us to open the door and let Him move freely in us, and through us. I write down scriptures and put them all over my house so that my family and I can be reminded to speak them out loud and see the changes in our hearts, lives, and home.

I enjoy hearing my children reading these scriptures as they go about their day. I know that the more they read the Word of God, the more it will seep into their hearts and minds and fill their spirits. *"Start children off on the way they should go, and even when they are old they will not turn from it"* (Proverbs 22:6). I often remind myself of this verse because right now, while my children are young, this work may seem tedious and unfruitful, but when they're older, they'll remember all the wonderful, spiritual things I've poured into them.

Another seed we sow into our children is getting them into the church body regularly. At our church recently, we've held praise and prayer nights almost every night during the week, and we've embraced the challenge of bringing all our children to these events, multiple nights in a row. The reward for all of us is even greater than the challenge. One of my favourite verses comes from Ephesians 3:

> *Now to him who is able to do immeasurably more than all we ask or imagine, according to his power that is at work within us, to him be glory in the church and in Christ Jesus throughout all generations, for ever and ever! Amen.*
>
> —Ephesians 3:20–21

We give God all the glory, for we know He is at work within us and wants to pour out so much upon us.

Because we made these nights a fun, routine "break" for our kids, they really enjoyed them, too. It was nice for them to be in a different environment and be surrounded by our faith community for many days in a row. Many of them got to know our children more, in good and very real, honest ways. That's life, and we're real people who have real kids.

These praise and prayer nights were also good for me to break out of the regular homework, dinner, and bedtime routine. The kids were excited to go out to the church, so they were motivated to get their homework done right after school. We were also able to enjoy some takeout dinners sometimes, which was a bonus. And because the evenings went a bit late, we could get the kids into bed as soon as we got home; everyone was tired and would sleep right away. I believe that if our children didn't have that early bedtime routine, this wouldn't have been so beneficial for us. But because we left the church near their bedtime, it was easy to get them all asleep afterward.

Making church a fun place for the family to be is important. Our attitudes can play out on our children, and how we feel toward the church and ministry will reflect on them.

Our family has four pastor's kids, or PKs, and my husband and I are constantly aware of the expectations others may have on our family and children. We never want our kids to be pressured by others' expectations, but to have their own authentic understanding of what God expects of them.

My prayer for my children is that they would run after God with all their hearts, and that the example my husband and I give them would show how important that is.

chapter eight

Teachable Moments

I OFTEN LAUGH AT MOMENTS NOW THAT USED TO SEEM RIDICULOUS. When my children are acting out and expressing themselves in ways that are completely outrageous (according to me), those are times when I now notice God speaking to me.

As Christians, we sometimes forget that we're children of God. The more I pay attention to the relationship I have with my children, the more I realize my relationship with God is so similar. I ask God to teach me about Him in very simple, practical ways and He uses my children as teaching tools many times.

One beautiful sunny day, my husband and I decided on the way home from grocery shopping with the kids that we would surprise them and get ice cream. Well, apparently the first thing we did wrong is wanting to keep it a surprise, so when we passed our street, there was an immediate uproar. In a loving but excited voice, we explained that we were taking them somewhere fun and they were going to love it. That was not enough for my oldest, who needs to have everything planned out. He proceeded to ask us a million questions, paving the way for his siblings to do the same. With each red light, this "wonderful surprise" was not feeling so wonderful anymore.

I began to regret this idea and became annoyed that we picked a place that seemed so far away. Our intentions were to bless them;

they love ice cream. After trying our best to avoid becoming too frustrated with them, we finally pulled into the ice cream store, and the van fell silent. The silence quickly turned into screams of excitement. It was so beautiful to see their glowing eyes and happy faces as we enjoyed this time together. It was so nice to hear them all give us thanks and sing songs all the way home. We didn't have a hard time convincing them that trusting us is a good thing to do.

This was absolutely a moment of reflection. God has great plans for our lives, but often we don't see the big picture, just the promise. Our surprise for our children was a promise that we made to them. We love them so much and always want to bless them, just like God loves us so much and is good to us. When we finally see the good that's going on, we're grateful and we come to understand that He's a loving Father who gives us His best.

Complaining seems to come first nature to all of us, but as we grow in our walk with Christ, we must choose to trust and *know* God is up to something great in our lives. We can live in peace and joy with thankful hearts; we reflect God's goodness.

> When we finally see the good that's going on, we're grateful and we come to understand that He's a loving Father who gives us His best.

I remember another time at home when I needed a moment to prepare to speak at church. I was running the midweek service that evening, excited to sit down and write out my message. Just as I was mid-thought and into my preparations, my toddler awoke from his nap and began to scream from his bed. I dropped all my notes and ran to him. He continued to scream when he saw me, and his tone told me that he was just mad (not hurt or sick) and didn't want me around. So I left his room and let him sit there and throw a tantrum on his bed. I assumed that something had woken him up and that he'd eventually fall back asleep.

I continued my preparations, taking notes and talking with God, but at this point, I was talking out loud (and loudly), so I could hear myself over my dear screaming child. But he didn't let up. I began to go through scriptures about loving the Lord your God and loving others as yourself, trying hard to concentrate and meditate.

I could feel my frustration starting to bubble. *What am I going to do with this child?* I wondered. *Do I punish him somehow for throwing this tantrum, when I know he's just tired but won't let me console him?* After another minute of God speaking to me about love and my annoyance getting the better of me, I stormed over to his room. My son still looked and sounded the same. I pointed at him, and in a loud voice that I know was God's and not my own, I exclaimed, "I love you!" Then I turned around and walked out of his room.

After I sat back down and got out my books yet again, I noticed that the crying stopped. Then I heard him use the washroom and flush the toilet. He came to me, happy. He had woken up early from his nap because he was uncomfortable and had to use the washroom. Screaming about it wasn't going to change how he felt, but getting up and taking care of the problem did.

That very night at church, I preached about the lesson I learned during that frustrating afternoon. As Christians, how many times do we throw our own fits when we feel the pressure mounting in our lives and it becomes uncomfortable? Meanwhile, the answer is right there, and has always been there. Even when we are at our most frustrated, God keeps reminding us that *He loves us.*

Sometimes I think God must laugh at us, the way I sometimes laugh when my children are having a tantrum because it's literally for no reason. We can be like that, too; a little silly at times. Our heavenly Father has everything we need to relieve that pressure we might be feeling, but it's up to us to take the steps that get us there.

We surprised our children another time by taking them to a small carnival nearby. As we were getting ready to leave the house, the excitement and fifty questions began. But the oldest remembered that we had driven past the carnival grounds a few days prior and had asked if we could go on the weekend, so the children were already expecting that we were going to go there. We had to first stop at the bank, where we could see the carnival. The children, hoping but unsure, continued to ask and even beg us to go.

Yet as we pulled into the nearby parking lot, they still were unsure, which surprised me a little. We parked right beside it, got out, and began to walk toward the rides, but the children were questioning and wanted to confirm with us that we were actually going where they were hoping to go.

We ended up having a wonderful time. The kids were so happy and excited, enjoying all the rides, games, and food. On the way home, my husband turned to me and said, "Listen to them; they're so happy talking about the carnival." All day long, the children kept thanking us and telling everyone they saw where they'd gone. That's what we desire to hear as parents. It blesses us so much when our children are happy. Do you know that it blesses God when He sees

His children happy and hears their gratitude, telling others of all His goodness?

As I thought about that day, I saw God's hand in it all. As His children, how often do we pray and ask God for something, yet as He leads us right toward it, we still question if it's sincerely for us? God brings us to a place where the answer is right in front of us, where He's obviously answered our prayer, yet we're unsure if He's truly going to follow through. I think that's because we're not used to expecting God's goodness in our lives. We pray, but do we expect God to answer those prayers, every time?

Sometimes in our Christian walk, our actions do resemble those of a child. We're told to have childlike faith. That's faith that believes in what God promises and expects them to happen.

> *"Jesus said, 'Let the little children come to me, and do not hinder them, for the kingdom of heaven belongs to such as these.'"*
>
> —Matthew 19:14

chapter nine

Vision

WHAT IS THE VISION YOU HAVE FOR YOUR CHILDREN, FAMILY, AND FOR yourself? Because what you see is what you'll get.

My children are growing up in a world that will dictate to them their future if I don't. I sometimes feel overwhelmed with this task, but I realize that all I have to do is my best, and God will do the rest.

I want my children to know that God has great plans for their future (Jeremiah 29:11). I want my children to know that they never have to worry about their life or where to find provision; all they need is a relationship with God, and He will lead and guide them, and even when things seem out of control, God is taking care of them always.

"Look at the birds of the air; they do not sow or reap or store away in barns, and yet your heavenly Father feeds them. Are you not much more valuable than they?" (Matthew 6:26). I want my children to know that no dream is impossible with God. *"Jesus looked at them and said, 'With man this is impossible, but with God all things are possible'"* (Matthew 19:26). Philippians 4:13 says, *"I can do all this through him who gives me strength."*

I want them to know that God never leaves them (Deuteronomy 31:6) and that when they pray, He hears their prayers and answers them (I John 5:14–15). I want them to love God and one another, for those are the greatest commandments. Their lives will be so blessed.

As parents, we must prioritize this and be aware of it every day. When they go to school or when they're at home, our children are being shaped into whom God created them to be. I'll say it again—it absolutely takes a village to raise a child. It's important that I make good choices for my children. Where they go to school, with whom they spend their time, or what they can or can't do on social media are all choices I make for them.

Parents, let's confidently take a stand for our children. We love them and we will guide them in the right direction. This doesn't mean that others who choose differently from me are wrong, but rather they're just not raising my child. They're raising their own.

The vision I have for my family is to have a healthy bond with each other. We show our love to one another by listening and encouraging. We pray our home to be a safe haven for us and open and welcome to all our extended family and friends—and our children's friends, too.

I envision our family enjoying each other's company. We can have fun on vacations far away as well as close to home. We can enjoy days out on field trips, but also time spent at home together, in the regular, everyday routines.

Our family is a powerful unit in the body of Christ. *"For where two or three gather in my name, there am I with them"* (Matthew 18:20). I want to see my family praying, moving mountains together. At the stage my children are right now, it's often difficult to get them through their bedtime prayers without losing focus (playing or fighting). But when they're touched by the Spirit and pray simple prayers, they're powerful. They're in full faith. They believe what they're saying and expect it to happen.

My family is the most important unit that will carry on the mighty power of God inside and outside our home. This is the main reason that Satan tries to break up families and create disunity, offense, and confusion. Parents, we must stand up and recognize the enemy's lies and bring God's freedom into our homes and families. *"The thief comes only to steal and kill and destroy; I have come that they may have life, and have it to the full"* (John 10:10).

I can't think of a better way to end this book than by helping you develop a vision for yourself. It's often easy, and sometimes expected, to put our children and spouses ahead of ourselves and our own needs, but this can become a burden rather than a blessing. I encourage you to take a moment and dream. Dream about *you!*

> YOU MIGHT HAVE THOUGHT YOU'RE MISSING OUT ON SOMETHING, BUT WHEN YOU GET RID OF THAT THOUGHT AND REPLACE IT WITH GOD TAKING YOU TO EVEN GREATER PLACES AND GIVING YOU EVEN BIGGER DREAMS THAN YOU HAD BEFORE, YOU'LL RISE UP EXCITED FOR EVERY NEW DAY.

What would you like to see for yourself? What would you like to accomplish this year or the next? What's something new that you would like to try? There might be something that you put on hold when you decided to start your family. Or maybe you didn't plan to have your family when you did, and you feel like you missed out on something. I want to tell you that God knew everything from start to finish; nothing surprises Him. You might have thought you're missing out on something, but when you get rid of that thought and replace it with God taking you to even greater places and giving you even bigger dreams than you had before, you'll rise up excited for every new day.

One scripture that's so powerful to me is, *"Take delight in the Lord, and he will give you the desires of your heart"* (Psalm 37:4). When I take time to think about my own heart's desires, I have a hard time believing that God wants to give me all these things, but He wouldn't have said it if He didn't mean it. He just loves us that much. We always want to give our own children good things, so why wouldn't we believe that God, our Father, wants the same for us?

Please take the time to write down all your own personal goals and desires. I have learned to write these things down, with the scripture that confirms God's Word for me and to remind myself of them often. That's how we know that we're praying God's will for our lives. If it's something that's in His Word, then He means it for you and over your situation, too. *"Keep this Book of the Law always on your lips; meditate on it day and night, so that you may be careful to do everything written in it. Then you will be prosperous and successful"* (Joshua 1:8).

"Write the vision; make it plain on tablets, so he may run who reads it" (Habakkuk 2:2, ESV). This is why I encourage you to put up scripture verses all over your home, so that you see God's promise for you. I encourage you to put your dreams and goals somewhere, too, that you would be reminded of them daily. Thanking God for these things that you want to happen in your life and believing they will come true is true faith. *"And without faith it is impossible to please God, because anyone who comes to him must believe that he exists and that he rewards those who earnestly seek him"* (Hebrews 11:6).

You will see your dreams come true. Get in agreement with God's Word and believe that it's for you. Even if the circumstances around you don't line up at the moment, have patience—they will change.

Our family currently needs a bigger home. The one we have right now is a rental and I feel like we're bursting out of it. I can say that my family needs to have a bigger home, my kids need to have their own rooms, my husband needs to have his own space—but if I'm totally honest, I want a bigger home for *me,* too (a walk-in closet would be great).

I found a beautiful home that I would like to move into right now, and it's more, in every way, than I could ask, think, or imagine (Ephesians 3:20). So I thank God for it and receive it by faith. I wait patiently for it and take the steps God is leading me to take.

God created us to love Him and enjoy our life with Him. He gave us everything we need so we don't need to be worried or stressed, but can have hope in Him daily. He said He'll finish the good work He started in us (Philippians 1:6).

There are some days when I beg Him to finish the good work already, because I'm tired, both physically and emotionally. Those days are hard, but I'm getting better. If I'm to acknowledge God in all things, it may not always go my way, but He's working all things out for my good. *"And we know that in all things God works for the good of those who love him, who have been called according to his purpose"* (Romans 8:28).

I can only try my best every day—that's all God requires of me. I don't have to put unrealistic expectations on myself because I call myself a Christian. I'm a Christian because I believe Christ died for me and I choose to follow Him.

I'm optimistic and have big dreams and goals for my life and family that I work on every day, even in little ways. Although it might seem small and insignificant at the moment, the things we as parents do and think today will set us on our path of victory. Victory may come in the form of a potty-trained child, a small reading scholar, the amazing graduate at the podium, the child who's become a father or mother themselves, or you simply having peace of mind.

Trust in God, and trust in yourself.

You've been given the child(ren) you have in your care because God created them and has a purpose for all of you to carry out. He trusts in you. He knows you inside and out; nothing surprises Him about you. If you've felt like you've fallen off the right path or strayed from God, that doesn't mean He gives up on you. In fact, He's always knocking at your door, waiting for when you're ready to answer. He has blessings for you all throughout your journey. If you feel like you might have missed them, don't worry about them disappearing; God makes new ones available. He will guide you back on the right path.

God can use those messy moments in our lives to speak to us—maybe we'll learn to like, or even love, those crayons and crumbs.

Also by the Author

The Promised Child

978-1-4866-1649-7

Danrey and Christie Amoyo knew that they wanted to be parents, but when their happy announcement turned into the worst possible scenario they found out that becoming parents was not to be an easy path for them.

This book is a written testimony of how determination, coming from a new revelation of faith, can change lives. It will demonstrate that the promises we read about in the Bible are for us today, even if we don't yet know how they apply to the situations we're living through.

Be encouraged by the Amoyos' experience as, after years of heartbreak and loss, the Word becomes real and they put their faith first.